AI Innovations in Oil and Gas

Transforming Exploration and Production

Table of Contents

Chapter 1: Introduction to AI in Oil and Gas

Overview of the Oil and Gas Industry

The oil and gas industry is a cornerstone of the global economy, providing energy resources that power industries, transportation, and households. This sector is characterized by its complex operations, which include exploration, extraction, refining, and distribution of hydrocarbons. The processes involved require extensive engineering expertise and advanced technologies to navigate the challenges of resource discovery, environmental regulations, and market fluctuations. As global energy demands continue to rise, the industry faces the dual challenge of increasing production efficiency while minimizing environmental impact, necessitating innovations in technology and operational practices.

In recent years, the integration of artificial intelligence has emerged as a transformative force within the oil and gas sector. AI technologies are being leveraged to enhance various aspects of the industry, from exploration to production. By utilizing machine learning algorithms and data analytics, companies can analyze vast amounts of geological and operational data to identify potential drilling sites more accurately. This not only reduces the time and costs associated with exploration but also increases the likelihood of successful resource extraction. The application of AI in this phase is pivotal, enabling engineers and geoscientists to make informed decisions based on predictive models and simulations.

Another critical area where AI is making significant inroads is in predictive maintenance for oil rigs. Traditional maintenance strategies often rely on scheduled checks and reactive measures, which can lead to unplanned downtime and costly repairs. AI-driven predictive maintenance utilizes sensors and data analytics to monitor equipment health in real-time, allowing operators to anticipate failures before they occur. This proactive approach enhances operational efficiency, reduces maintenance costs, and extends the lifespan of expensive drilling equipment. Engineers can implement these AI tools to streamline maintenance schedules and improve safety protocols, thus enhancing overall productivity on-site.

Drilling optimization is another domain benefiting from AI innovations. Advanced algorithms can analyze historical drilling data to identify optimal drilling parameters, thereby improving efficiency and reducing the risk of costly errors. By simulating various drilling scenarios, AI can help engineers optimize bit selection, drilling fluids, and even well trajectory. This level of precision not only leads to better resource recovery rates but also minimizes the environmental footprint of drilling operations. As AI continues to evolve, its role in refining drilling techniques will be crucial for achieving higher production levels while adhering to sustainability practices.

Enhanced oil recovery (EOR) techniques are also being transformed through AI applications. Traditional EOR methods often involve complex chemical processes and extensive energy inputs. AI can optimize these processes by analyzing subsurface data and predicting how fluids will interact with different reservoir conditions. Machine learning models can assist in selecting the most effective EOR strategies, ultimately improving recovery rates and reducing operational costs. The convergence of AI with EOR technologies represents a significant advancement in the quest for maximizing hydrocarbon extraction while minimizing environmental impacts, aligning with the industry's broader goals of sustainability and efficiency.

The Role of Technology in Industry Evolution

The integration of technology in the oil and gas industry has significantly reshaped its operational landscape, driving efficiency, safety, and sustainability. With the advent of Artificial Intelligence (AI), the sector has witnessed transformative changes that optimize exploration and production processes. AI has enabled engineers and scientists to analyze vast datasets, leading to more informed decision-making. This evolution is not merely a trend; it is a fundamental shift that enhances the industry's ability to respond to challenges while maximizing resource recovery.

Predictive maintenance is one of the most critical advancements facilitated by AI technologies. By leveraging machine learning algorithms and real-time data analytics, operators can predict equipment failures before they occur. This proactive approach reduces downtime and maintenance costs, leading to increased operational efficiency. Engineers can monitor vital parameters of oil rigs, identifying anomalies that indicate potential issues. Consequently, the implementation of predictive maintenance not only improves reliability but also extends the lifespan of equipment, which is a crucial aspect of resource management in oil and gas operations.

AI-driven exploration has further revolutionized the search for new reserves. Traditional methods of exploration are often time-consuming and costly, relying heavily on geological surveys and drilling trials. However, AI enhances these processes by analyzing geological data, seismic readings, and historical drilling information to identify potential drilling locations with higher success rates. The adoption of AI algorithms allows scientists to iterate quickly through multiple scenarios, evaluating the feasibility of various sites and reducing the risk associated with new exploration ventures. This efficiency not only accelerates the exploration phase but also contributes to more sustainable resource management.

Drilling optimization is another area where AI has made a significant impact. The use of AI technologies enables real-time monitoring and adjustment of drilling parameters. Engineers can analyze data from multiple sensors installed on drilling rigs to optimize drilling performance, minimizing costs while maximizing output. The ability to adapt drilling strategies based on real-time feedback ensures that operations remain efficient and effective under varying conditions. This dynamic approach not only enhances productivity but also contributes to safer drilling practices, as operators can make informed adjustments to mitigate risks.

Enhanced oil recovery techniques have also benefited from AI innovations. Traditional methods of oil recovery often leave significant amounts of crude oil in the reservoir, but AI technologies facilitate improved extraction processes. By utilizing advanced modeling and simulation techniques, engineers can better understand reservoir behavior and apply targeted recovery methods. AI-driven insights allow for the identification of optimal injection strategies and the management of reservoir pressure, leading to increased recovery rates. As the industry seeks to balance profitability with environmental responsibility, these AI-enhanced techniques play a vital role in maximizing resource extraction while minimizing ecological impact.

Introduction to Artificial Intelligence

Artificial Intelligence (AI) has emerged as a transformative force across numerous industries, and the oil and gas sector is no exception. With the increasing complexity of operations, the volatile nature of market dynamics, and the growing emphasis on sustainability, the integration of AI technologies offers unprecedented opportunities for enhancing efficiency, safety, and profitability in exploration and production activities. This subchapter aims to provide engineers and scientists with a foundational understanding of AI and its applications within the oil and gas industry, highlighting the innovative practices that are reshaping traditional methodologies.

At its core, AI refers to the ability of machines to perform tasks that typically require human intelligence, such as reasoning, learning, and problem-solving. In the context of oil and gas, AI encompasses a range of technologies, including machine learning, natural language processing, and computer vision, which can analyze vast amounts of data to extract actionable insights. The power of AI lies in its ability to process and interpret data at speeds and accuracies far beyond human capabilities, enabling companies to make informed decisions based on real-time information. This capability is particularly critical in an industry where data from various sources, such as sensors, geological surveys, and historical records, must be continuously analyzed to optimize operations.

One of the most significant applications of AI in oil and gas is predictive maintenance, which leverages data analytics to anticipate equipment failures before they occur. By using machine learning algorithms to analyze historical maintenance data and real-time sensor readings, companies can identify patterns that indicate potential issues. This proactive approach to maintenance not only reduces downtime and operational costs but also enhances safety by minimizing the risk of accidents related to equipment failure. Engineers and scientists can develop models that predict when maintenance should be performed, extending the lifespan of equipment and ensuring a more reliable production process.

AI-driven exploration and drilling optimization represent another critical area where artificial intelligence is making substantial inroads. Traditional exploration methods often involve considerable time and resources, with significant uncertainties regarding the viability of drilling sites. AI technologies can analyze geological data, seismic surveys, and production histories to identify high-potential drilling locations more accurately. Machine learning algorithms can optimize drilling parameters in real-time, adapting to subsurface conditions as they change. This capability not only increases the success rate of exploration efforts but also reduces the environmental impact by minimizing unnecessary drilling activities.

Enhanced oil recovery techniques utilizing AI are also gaining traction as companies seek to maximize output from existing fields. By employing AI to analyze reservoir behavior and fluid dynamics, operators can develop more effective recovery strategies. Machine learning models can simulate various recovery scenarios, helping engineers to identify the most efficient methods for extracting oil while considering economic and environmental factors. As the industry faces the dual challenges of declining reserves and increased regulatory scrutiny, the integration of AI into recovery processes will be crucial for sustaining production levels and achieving long-term viability.

Chapter 2: The Power of AI in Oil and Gas

Understanding AI Technologies

Artificial Intelligence (AI) encompasses a range of technologies that enable machines to simulate human intelligence processes. In the oil and gas sector, these technologies significantly enhance decision-making, operational efficiency, and safety. Engineers and scientists in this field are leveraging machine learning, natural language processing, and data analytics to innovate and optimize various processes. Machine learning algorithms analyze large datasets to identify patterns and predict outcomes, while natural language processing helps in interpreting data from unstructured sources, such as reports and logs. By understanding these core technologies, professionals can better appreciate their application in exploration and production.

Predictive maintenance is one of the most impactful applications of AI in oil rigs. Using AI algorithms, organizations can predict equipment failures before they occur by analyzing historical data, sensor readings, and operational metrics. This proactive approach allows for timely interventions, reducing downtime and maintenance costs. For instance, predictive models can forecast when critical components, such as pumps or compressors, are likely to fail, enabling maintenance teams to perform repairs during planned downtime. This not only improves the reliability of operations but also extends the lifespan of equipment, leading to significant cost savings in the long run.

AI-driven exploration and drilling optimization represent another frontier where AI technologies are making a substantial impact. Advanced algorithms can process geological data, historical drilling performance, and environmental factors to maximize drilling efficiency. By integrating AI with geographic information systems (GIS) and other data sources, engineers can identify optimal drilling locations and strategies. This capability minimizes risks associated with drilling, such as unexpected geological formations or environmental concerns, ultimately enhancing the success rates of exploration efforts. The ability to make data-driven decisions in real time is transforming how companies approach exploration and drilling.

Enhanced oil recovery techniques are also being revolutionized by AI applications. Traditional methods of enhanced oil recovery often involve trial-and-error approaches, leading to inefficiencies and increased costs. AI technologies can analyze complex reservoir data and simulate various recovery scenarios to identify the most effective techniques. For example, machine learning models can predict how reservoirs will respond to different methods, such as water flooding or gas injection, allowing engineers to select optimal strategies based on specific reservoir characteristics. This targeted approach not only improves recovery rates but also minimizes environmental impacts associated with oil extraction.

In conclusion, the integration of AI technologies in the oil and gas sector is transforming exploration and production processes. By understanding and leveraging these technologies, engineers and scientists can drive innovation and achieve greater efficiencies. As the industry continues to evolve, staying informed about advancements in AI will be crucial for professionals seeking to enhance their operational capabilities and contribute to sustainable practices in oil and gas exploration and production.

Case Studies of AI Implementation

The implementation of artificial intelligence in the oil and gas sector has led to notable case studies that exemplify the transformative potential of this technology. One significant case is the deployment of predictive maintenance systems on offshore oil rigs. Companies have integrated machine learning algorithms to analyze data from sensors embedded in equipment. These systems can predict potential failures before they occur, enabling proactive maintenance that minimizes downtime and reduces operational costs. For instance, a major oil company reported a 20% reduction in unplanned outages after implementing an AI-driven predictive maintenance program, highlighting the role of AI in enhancing operational efficiency.

Another compelling example is the use of AI in exploration and drilling optimization. Advanced analytics and deep learning models have been employed to process vast amounts of geological and seismic data, improving the accuracy of reservoir characterization. A consortium of energy firms utilized AI algorithms to analyze historical drilling data alongside real-time measurements. This approach enabled them to optimize drilling parameters dynamically, resulting in a 15% increase in drilling success rates. The ability to leverage AI for more precise decision-making in drilling operations not only accelerates project timelines but also significantly reduces costs associated with exploration.

Enhanced oil recovery techniques have also seen significant advancements through AI applications. Companies have begun employing AI to model and simulate various recovery scenarios, allowing for the identification of the most effective methods to extract additional oil from existing reservoirs. In one case, an operator utilized reinforcement learning algorithms to optimize waterflooding strategies, which led to a 10% increase in recovery rates. This case illustrates how AI can facilitate smarter resource management and improve the economics of oil recovery operations in mature fields.

AI's role in environmental monitoring and risk assessment is another critical aspect of its implementation in the oil and gas industry. One notable case involved the use of AI-driven analytics to monitor environmental impacts in real-time at drilling sites. By analyzing data from satellite imagery and ground sensors, companies were able to detect and respond to potential environmental hazards more effectively. This proactive approach not only ensures compliance with regulatory standards but also enhances the public image of the company by demonstrating a commitment to sustainable practices.

Finally, the integration of AI into supply chain management and logistics within the oil and gas sector has proven to be beneficial. Companies have adopted AI algorithms to analyze market trends, optimize inventory levels, and streamline transportation logistics. In a recent implementation, an oil major reported that AI-driven supply chain optimization led to a 25% reduction in logistics costs. This case highlights how AI can enhance overall operational efficiencies while ensuring that resources are allocated intelligently across the supply chain, ultimately contributing to a more resilient and responsive industry.

Benefits of AI in Enhancing Operational Efficiency

The integration of artificial intelligence (AI) in the oil and gas sector has emerged as a transformative force, particularly in enhancing operational efficiency. By leveraging advanced data analytics, machine learning algorithms, and real-time monitoring, AI solutions streamline processes, reduce downtime, and optimize resource allocation. This not only leads to cost savings but also significantly improves productivity across various operational facets, from exploration to production.

Predictive maintenance is one of the most impactful applications of AI in oil rigs. By utilizing machine learning models that analyze historical and real-time data from equipment, operators can predict potential failures before they occur. This proactive approach minimizes unplanned outages and extends the lifespan of critical machinery. For engineers and scientists, the ability to forecast maintenance needs translates into more efficient scheduling of repairs and reduced operational disruptions, ultimately leading to improved safety and enhanced productivity at drilling sites.

AI-driven exploration techniques further contribute to operational efficiency by optimizing drilling processes and resource identification. Advanced geospatial analysis and predictive analytics allow engineers to assess geological data more accurately, identifying high-potential drilling sites with greater precision. This reduces the time and costs associated with exploratory drilling while increasing the likelihood of successful outcomes. The ability to rapidly process vast amounts of geological and seismic data ensures that decision-making is data-driven and aligns with the latest technological advancements.

In terms of enhanced oil recovery techniques, AI plays a pivotal role in optimizing recovery processes. Machine learning algorithms can analyze complex reservoir data to develop tailored recovery strategies that maximize output while minimizing environmental impact. By simulating various recovery scenarios and analyzing the resulting data, engineers can implement more effective extraction methods. This not only boosts production rates but also contributes to more sustainable practices within the industry, aligning operational efficiency with environmental stewardship.

The cumulative effect of integrating AI across these operational facets is a significant enhancement in overall efficiency for oil and gas companies. By automating routine tasks, improving predictive capabilities, and enabling data-driven decision-making, organizations can achieve higher operational standards. For engineers and scientists in the field, embracing AI technologies presents an opportunity to not only optimize current practices but also to innovate future methodologies, ensuring the industry remains competitive in an increasingly complex energy landscape.

Chapter 3: Predictive Maintenance in Oil Rigs

Importance of Predictive Maintenance

Predictive maintenance is revolutionizing the oil and gas industry by significantly reducing downtime and enhancing operational efficiency. Through advanced data analytics and machine learning algorithms, predictive maintenance enables engineers to anticipate equipment failures before they occur. By continuously monitoring the condition of machinery such as pumps, compressors, and drilling rigs, organizations can make informed decisions about when to perform maintenance. This proactive approach not only minimizes unexpected breakdowns but also optimizes the utilization of resources, thereby improving overall productivity in exploration and production operations.

The application of predictive maintenance techniques is particularly critical in oil rigs, where the harsh operating environment can lead to rapid wear and tear on equipment. By employing sensors and IoT technologies, engineers can gather real-time data on various parameters such as temperature, pressure, and vibration. This data is then analyzed using AI algorithms to identify patterns and potential failure modes. As a result, maintenance teams can schedule interventions at the most opportune times, reducing the risk of catastrophic failures that can lead to costly operational disruptions and safety hazards.

Moreover, the integration of predictive maintenance within AI-driven exploration and drilling optimization frameworks enhances decision-making processes. When engineers can forecast maintenance needs accurately, they are better equipped to plan drilling schedules and resource allocation effectively. This synergy not only streamlines operations but also contributes to more precise drilling outcomes, reducing the likelihood of drilling inefficiencies and improving the overall success rate of exploration efforts. The ability to mitigate risks associated with equipment failure thus becomes a fundamental aspect of optimizing drilling operations in the oil and gas sector.

Enhanced oil recovery techniques further benefit from predictive maintenance strategies. For instance, the performance of injection pumps and compressors is critical in maintaining optimal reservoir pressure. By predicting potential malfunctions in these key components, companies can ensure that enhanced oil recovery processes are not interrupted. This capability allows for sustained production levels and maximizes the extraction of hydrocarbons from existing fields, which is increasingly important as new discoveries become less frequent and the focus shifts to optimizing current assets.

In conclusion, the importance of predictive maintenance in the oil and gas industry cannot be overstated. By leveraging AI and advanced analytics, companies can transform their maintenance strategies from reactive to proactive, leading to significant improvements in operational efficiency, safety, and profitability. As the industry continues to embrace technological innovations, predictive maintenance will play a pivotal role in shaping the future of exploration and production, ensuring that organizations can meet the growing energy demands while minimizing environmental impacts.

AI Techniques for Predictive Maintenance

Predictive maintenance in the oil and gas industry has been revolutionized by artificial intelligence techniques, significantly enhancing operational efficiency and minimizing downtime. Traditional maintenance methods, which often rely on scheduled inspections, can lead to unnecessary costs and equipment failures. By integrating AI-driven predictive maintenance strategies, companies can analyze vast amounts of operational data in real time to predict equipment failures before they occur. This proactive approach not only reduces the risk of unplanned outages but also extends the lifespan of critical assets, ultimately saving costs and improving overall productivity.

Machine learning algorithms play a crucial role in predictive maintenance by identifying patterns in historical data. These algorithms can process data from various sources, including sensors on drilling rigs, maintenance logs, and environmental conditions. By training on past performance metrics, machine learning models can detect anomalies that signal potential failures. For instance, a sudden increase in vibration from a pump may indicate an impending mechanical issue. By recognizing such patterns early, engineers can schedule maintenance activities at opportune times, thereby minimizing disruptions to operations.

Another significant AI technique utilized in predictive maintenance is predictive analytics, which involves the use of statistical algorithms and machine learning models to analyze current and historical data. Predictive analytics can forecast equipment health and predict when maintenance should be performed to avoid failures. This technique allows for the optimization of maintenance schedules based on actual usage and condition rather than on a fixed timetable. By tailoring maintenance interventions to the actual state of equipment, companies can achieve a more efficient allocation of resources and reduce overall operational costs.

Deep learning, a subset of machine learning, further enhances predictive maintenance capabilities by enabling the analysis of unstructured data, such as images and text. In oil and gas operations, deep learning can be applied to visual inspection data and reports to identify potential issues. For example, image recognition algorithms can analyze photos from inspections of drilling equipment to detect wear or damage that may not be evident to the human eye. This capability allows for more thorough assessments and timely interventions, ensuring that equipment remains in optimal condition.

The integration of IoT (Internet of Things) devices with AI techniques amplifies the effectiveness of predictive maintenance in oil and gas. IoT sensors can continuously monitor equipment conditions and relay data to AI systems for analysis. This real-time data collection enables engineers to maintain an up-to-date understanding of equipment performance and health. By leveraging the power of AI coupled with IoT technologies, companies can not only predict failures with greater accuracy but also implement maintenance strategies that enhance safety and reliability across their operations, leading to improved productivity and reduced environmental impact.

Real-world Applications and Success Stories

Real-world applications of artificial intelligence in the oil and gas sector have demonstrated significant advancements, particularly in enhancing operational efficiency and driving cost reductions. One notable example is the implementation of predictive maintenance in oil rigs. By utilizing machine learning algorithms to analyze historical data from equipment sensors, companies have been able to anticipate failures before they occur. This proactive approach minimizes downtime, reduces maintenance costs, and extends the lifespan of critical assets. Companies leveraging AI-driven predictive maintenance have reported reductions in unplanned outages by as much as 30%, illustrating a compelling case for the technology's integration into standard operational procedures.

In the realm of exploration, AI has revolutionized the way geoscientists identify and evaluate potential drilling sites. Traditional methods often rely on extensive geological surveys and seismic data interpretation, which can be time-consuming and prone to human error. However, AI algorithms can process vast amounts of data more quickly and accurately, identifying patterns and anomalies that might be missed by human analysts. For instance, companies employing AI-driven exploration techniques have successfully reduced exploration timeframes by up to 50%, allowing for faster decision-making and more efficient resource allocation. This rapid assessment capability enables firms to focus their efforts on the most promising areas, significantly increasing the likelihood of successful drilling operations.

Drilling optimization is another area where AI has made a significant impact. By analyzing real-time data from drilling operations, machine learning models can provide recommendations for adjusting parameters such as weight on bit, rotation speed, and mud properties. These adjustments can lead to improved rate of penetration and reduced drilling costs. Operators using AI-enhanced drilling optimization have reported savings of up to 20% in drilling costs, along with improved safety outcomes due to enhanced monitoring of drilling conditions. The ability to continuously learn from operational data further empowers teams to refine their strategies over time, cementing the role of AI as a vital tool in modern drilling practices.

Enhanced oil recovery techniques have also benefited from AI advancements. Traditional methods of increasing oil extraction often involve complex chemical processes or physical interventions that can be costly and environmentally challenging. AI applications can optimize these recovery processes by predicting the most effective methods based on reservoir characteristics and historical performance data. For example, companies have successfully employed AI to model fluid dynamics within reservoirs, leading to more efficient injection strategies. The results have been promising, with some operators achieving increases in recovery rates of up to 10%, thus maximizing the return on investment for existing fields.

Success stories across the industry serve as powerful testimonials to the transformative potential of AI in oil and gas. From improved predictive maintenance practices to enhanced exploration and drilling optimization, the integration of AI technologies is reshaping the operational landscape. These innovations not only drive profitability but also contribute to more sustainable practices within the sector. As engineers and scientists continue to explore new frontiers in AI applications, the oil and gas industry stands poised to reap the benefits of advanced technologies, ensuring its evolution in an increasingly competitive and environmentally conscious world.

Chapter 4: AI-Driven Exploration and Drilling Optimization

Traditional vs. AI-Enhanced Exploration

The landscape of oil and gas exploration has undergone a significant transformation with the advent of artificial intelligence (AI). Traditional exploration methods, which have relied heavily on geological surveys, seismic data interpretation, and human expertise, often involve extensive time and labor. Engineers and scientists have employed these conventional techniques to identify potential drilling sites and assess reservoir viability. However, the limitations of human analysis, including biases and the inability to process vast datasets efficiently, have prompted the industry to seek innovative solutions. As a result, AI-enhanced exploration has emerged as a powerful alternative, capable of processing complex information at unprecedented speeds and providing insights that were previously unattainable.

AI technologies, such as machine learning and data analytics, have revolutionized how geoscientists approach exploration. By leveraging large datasets from various sources, including satellite imagery, geological maps, and seismic readings, AI algorithms can identify patterns and correlations that human analysts might overlook. This capability not only improves the accuracy of site selection but also reduces the time required to evaluate potential drilling locations. Furthermore, AI can continuously learn from new data, allowing for ongoing refinement of exploration strategies. This adaptability is crucial in an industry where conditions can change rapidly and new information can significantly alter drilling plans.

Predictive maintenance is another critical area where AI is enhancing traditional practices in oil rigs. In conventional setups, maintenance schedules are often reactive, based on equipment failure or extensive wear-and-tear assessments. AI-driven predictive maintenance, on the other hand, utilizes real-time monitoring and historical data analysis to anticipate equipment failures before they occur. By analyzing patterns in machinery performance, AI can identify potential issues and suggest timely interventions, thereby minimizing downtime and optimizing operational efficiency. This proactive approach not only extends the life of equipment but also contributes to safer working conditions on oil rigs.

Drilling optimization is yet another domain where AI is making significant strides. Traditional drilling practices often involve trial-and-error methods, which can lead to inefficiencies and increased costs. AI-enhanced drilling optimization utilizes advanced algorithms to analyze drilling parameters in real-time, allowing engineers to make informed adjustments on the fly. These systems can evaluate factors such as torque, weight on bit, and rate of penetration, providing recommendations that enhance drilling performance. The result is a more efficient drilling process that not only reduces operational costs but also minimizes the environmental impact associated with exploration activities.

Finally, enhanced oil recovery techniques are benefiting from AI innovations in substantial ways. Traditional methods of oil recovery often leave a significant amount of hydrocarbons unrecovered due to inefficiencies in the extraction process. AI technologies enable a more sophisticated understanding of reservoir dynamics, allowing for the development of tailored recovery strategies. By simulating different recovery scenarios and analyzing the outcomes, AI can inform decisions on the most effective methods to extract oil. This integration of AI in enhanced oil recovery not only maximizes resource extraction but also supports the industry's transition toward more sustainable practices, ensuring that more oil can be recovered with less environmental impact.

Machine Learning in Drilling Optimization

Machine learning has emerged as a transformative technology in drilling optimization, fundamentally changing how oil and gas companies approach exploration and production. By leveraging vast amounts of data generated during drilling operations, machine learning algorithms can identify patterns and correlations that human analysts might overlook. This capability allows for the development of models that can predict drilling performance, enhance decision-making, and improve overall operational efficiency. The integration of machine learning into drilling processes not only reduces costs but also minimizes risks associated with exploration in challenging environments.

One of the key applications of machine learning in drilling optimization is predictive maintenance. By analyzing historical data from drilling rigs, machine learning algorithms can predict equipment failures before they occur, allowing for timely maintenance interventions. This proactive approach not only extends the lifespan of drilling equipment but also prevents costly downtime that can arise from unexpected breakdowns. Engineers can leverage these insights to optimize maintenance schedules, ensuring that rigs remain operational and efficient, thus maximizing productivity and reducing operational costs in oil and gas extraction.

Furthermore, machine learning enhances the planning and execution of drilling operations through real-time data analysis. Advanced algorithms can process data from various sensors and systems on drilling rigs, providing insights into drilling parameters such as rate of penetration, torque, and bit wear. By continuously monitoring these parameters, machine learning can help engineers make informed adjustments during the drilling process, optimizing performance based on real-time conditions. This adaptability leads to reduced drilling times and improved wellbore quality, ultimately contributing to better resource recovery.

Another significant benefit of machine learning in drilling optimization is its ability to improve well placement and trajectory planning. By analyzing geological and historical drilling data, machine learning models can identify optimal drilling paths that enhance resource recovery while minimizing risks. These models consider various factors, including rock properties, fluid dynamics, and historical drilling outcomes, enabling engineers to make data-driven decisions about where to drill and how to navigate complex geological formations. This precision not only increases the likelihood of successful drilling but also helps in maximizing the extraction of hydrocarbons from reservoirs.

In conclusion, the integration of machine learning into drilling optimization represents a significant advancement for the oil and gas industry. By harnessing the power of AI to analyze data, predict equipment failures, optimize drilling parameters, and enhance well placement, engineers and scientists can drive efficiency and productivity in exploration and production activities. As the industry continues to evolve, the adoption of machine learning will play a crucial role in overcoming the challenges associated with drilling in increasingly complex environments, ultimately leading to more sustainable and profitable operations.

Impact on Cost and Time Efficiency

The integration of artificial intelligence (AI) in the oil and gas sector has significantly influenced cost and time efficiency across various operations. With predictive analytics, companies can now leverage data to anticipate equipment failures before they occur, reducing downtime and maintenance costs. By analyzing historical performance data, AI systems predict when specific components are likely to fail, allowing for timely interventions. This shift from reactive to proactive maintenance not only extends the lifespan of equipment but also minimizes unplanned outages, which can be costly and disruptive to production schedules.

In exploration and drilling, AI-driven technologies enhance the decision-making process by providing real-time data analysis and insights. Machine learning algorithms can process vast amounts of geological and seismic data rapidly, identifying patterns and anomalies that may indicate the presence of oil or gas reserves. This accelerates the exploration phase, allowing companies to make informed decisions more quickly and efficiently. The automation of data interpretation reduces the need for extensive manual analysis, leading to a significant decrease in exploration timelines and associated costs.

Drilling optimization through AI also plays a critical role in improving cost efficiency. By utilizing AI algorithms to analyze drilling parameters and performance data, companies can optimize drilling practices to achieve faster penetration rates while minimizing wear and tear on equipment. Advanced AI models can simulate various drilling scenarios, helping engineers select the most effective strategies for specific geological conditions. This optimization not only shortens the drilling process but also reduces fuel consumption and associated operational costs, making drilling operations more sustainable.

Enhanced oil recovery (EOR) techniques have also benefited from AI innovations, leading to improved recovery rates and reduced costs. AI systems can analyze reservoir data to identify the most effective EOR methods tailored to specific conditions. By predicting how different recovery techniques will perform, companies can make better strategic decisions that maximize oil extraction while minimizing wastage. This targeted approach reduces the resources and time required for EOR projects, ultimately translating into lower operational expenses.

Overall, the impact of AI on cost and time efficiency in the oil and gas industry is profound. By streamlining operations, enhancing predictive maintenance, and optimizing exploration and recovery techniques, AI technologies are reshaping the landscape of oil and gas production. As engineers and scientists continue to explore the capabilities of AI, the potential for further advancements in operational efficiency and cost reduction remains promising, paving the way for a more sustainable and profitable industry.

Chapter 5: Enhanced Oil Recovery Techniques Using AI

Overview of Enhanced Oil Recovery (EOR)

Enhanced Oil Recovery (EOR) refers to a variety of techniques employed to increase the amount of crude oil that can be extracted from an oil reservoir beyond what is achievable through primary and secondary recovery methods. Traditional recovery methods typically allow for the extraction of only about 20 to 40 percent of the total oil in place, leaving significant amounts unrecoverable. EOR aims to improve these extraction rates by utilizing advanced technologies and methodologies, which can include thermal recovery, gas injection, and chemical flooding. The implementation of EOR techniques is essential in maximizing resource utilization, optimizing production processes, and ultimately increasing the economic viability of oil fields.

One of the most significant advancements in EOR has been the integration of artificial intelligence (AI) technologies. AI plays a pivotal role in analyzing complex geological data, predicting reservoir behavior, and optimizing recovery strategies. Machine learning algorithms can process vast datasets to identify patterns and trends that might not be evident through conventional analysis. This capability allows engineers and scientists to make informed decisions about which EOR techniques to apply and how to deploy them effectively, minimizing risks and enhancing overall recovery rates.

Predictive maintenance is another critical application of AI within enhanced oil recovery. By leveraging real-time data from sensors and historical performance records, AI can predict equipment failures before they occur. This proactive approach not only reduces downtime but also ensures that EOR operations run smoothly and efficiently. Implementing predictive maintenance in oil rigs helps to maintain optimal performance levels, allowing for continuous production and reducing operational costs associated with unplanned repairs or shutdowns.

AI-driven exploration and drilling optimization also contribute significantly to the success of EOR initiatives. Advanced algorithms can analyze geological formations, assess drilling performance, and recommend optimal drilling techniques tailored to specific reservoirs. This optimization not only enhances initial recovery rates but also improves the overall efficiency of the extraction process. By focusing on data-driven methodologies, engineers can adapt their approaches to changing conditions in real-time, ensuring that EOR operations are both effective and sustainable.

In conclusion, enhanced oil recovery represents a crucial component of modern oil extraction practices, particularly as traditional resources dwindle and the demand for energy continues to grow. The integration of AI technologies into EOR processes is transforming how engineers and scientists approach the challenges associated with oil recovery. By harnessing the power of predictive maintenance, drilling optimization, and advanced data analytics, the industry is poised to unlock previously inaccessible oil reserves, ensuring a more sustainable and profitable future for oil and gas exploration and production.

AI Applications in EOR Strategies

AI applications in Enhanced Oil Recovery (EOR) strategies are transforming the way oil and gas companies approach resource extraction. Traditional EOR techniques, such as water flooding or gas injection, have been enhanced through the integration of AI technologies, which enable more precise control and optimization of these complex processes. By leveraging machine learning algorithms and advanced data analytics, engineers can analyze vast amounts of geological, operational, and production data to identify the most effective EOR methods tailored to specific reservoirs. This data-driven approach minimizes risks and maximizes recovery rates, ultimately leading to increased profitability for oil and gas operators.

One significant application of AI in EOR is the use of predictive analytics to forecast reservoir behavior under various recovery scenarios. Machine learning models can analyze historical production data along with real-time sensor inputs to predict how changes in pressure, temperature, and fluid composition will impact oil recovery. By simulating different EOR strategies, engineers can identify optimal conditions for injecting fluids and adjust operations proactively. This predictive capability reduces trial-and-error approaches, allowing for more efficient planning and execution of EOR projects.

AI-driven optimization tools also play a crucial role in managing the complexities of EOR operations. These tools utilize algorithms that take into account numerous variables, such as reservoir characteristics, fluid properties, and operational constraints, to recommend optimal injection rates and patterns. Engineers can use these insights to fine-tune their strategies continuously, ensuring that EOR processes are not only effective but also environmentally sustainable. The integration of AI in monitoring and controlling EOR activities can lead to significant reductions in operational costs and improved overall efficiency.

Moreover, AI facilitates enhanced collaboration among multidisciplinary teams involved in EOR projects. By providing a centralized platform for data sharing and communication, AI technologies enable geologists, reservoir engineers, and production specialists to work together more effectively. This collaborative environment fosters innovation and allows teams to leverage diverse expertise in developing and implementing EOR strategies. The ability to visualize complex data and trends through AI-powered dashboards enhances decision-making processes, ensuring that all stakeholders are aligned and informed.

As the oil and gas industry continues to embrace digital transformation, the role of AI in EOR strategies will only grow. Future advancements in AI technology, such as more sophisticated neural networks and real-time data integration capabilities, will further enhance the precision of EOR techniques. Companies that invest in these innovations will likely gain a competitive edge, leading to improved recovery rates and reduced environmental impacts. The ongoing evolution of AI applications in EOR exemplifies the transformative potential of artificial intelligence in the oil and gas sector, marking a new era in exploration and production efficiency.

Future Directions for AI in EOR

As the oil and gas industry increasingly integrates artificial intelligence into its operations, the future of Enhanced Oil

Recovery (EOR) stands to benefit significantly from these advancements. One of the primary areas of growth is the application of machine learning algorithms to optimize EOR processes. By analyzing massive datasets from various sources, including geological surveys, production logs, and sensor readings, AI can identify patterns and correlations that may not be evident through traditional analysis. This capability allows for the more precise modeling of reservoir behavior and the prediction of recovery rates, ultimately leading to more efficient and cost-effective EOR strategies.

Predictive maintenance is another critical aspect where AI is expected to revolutionize EOR operations. By employing AI-driven analytics, companies can monitor equipment health in real-time, predicting failures before they occur. This proactive approach not only minimizes downtime but also enhances safety and extends the life of critical assets. For instance, machine learning models can analyze vibration data from pumps and compressors, identifying anomalies that signal potential malfunctions. As predictive maintenance becomes more sophisticated, it will facilitate the seamless integration of AI into daily operations, ensuring that EOR processes are not only efficient but also resilient.

AI-driven exploration and drilling optimization are poised to transform how oil and gas companies approach resource extraction. Advanced algorithms can process geological and seismic data more rapidly and accurately than ever before, enabling companies to identify promising drilling locations with higher confidence. This reduces the financial risk associated with exploratory drilling and enhances the overall yield from EOR projects. Moreover, AI can optimize drilling parameters in real time, adjusting drilling techniques based on feedback from sensors embedded in the drilling equipment. This adaptability ensures that drilling operations are conducted at optimal speeds and pressures, reducing costs and improving recovery rates.

The future of EOR will also see enhanced collaboration between human expertise and AI technologies. As engineers and scientists become more accustomed to working alongside AI systems, they will leverage these tools to augment their decision-making processes. The synergy between human intuition and AI's analytical capabilities can lead to breakthroughs in EOR techniques that were previously unattainable. Training and education programs focused on AI applications in EOR will be essential, allowing professionals to harness these technologies effectively and drive innovation within their organizations.

Finally, ethical considerations and regulatory frameworks will play a crucial role in shaping the future of AI in EOR. As companies adopt more advanced AI technologies, they must also address the implications of data privacy, algorithmic transparency, and environmental impact. The development of industry standards for AI application in EOR will be necessary to ensure responsible usage and to foster trust among stakeholders. By prioritizing ethical practices, the oil and gas industry can harness the full potential of AI in EOR while safeguarding its reputation and contributing to a more sustainable energy future.

Chapter 6: Challenges and Limitations of AI in Oil and Gas

Data Quality and Availability Issues

Data quality and availability are critical factors in maximizing the potential of artificial intelligence within the oil and gas sector. In the context of AI-driven exploration and drilling optimization, the reliance on high-quality data cannot be overstated. The effectiveness of machine learning algorithms hinges on the integrity of the datasets used for training. Inaccurate, incomplete, or outdated data can lead to faulty predictions and suboptimal decision-making, ultimately affecting operational efficiency and safety. Engineers and scientists must prioritize data validation processes to ensure that the information fed into AI systems is both accurate and relevant.

One of the significant challenges in achieving high data quality lies in the integration of diverse data sources. Oil and gas operations generate vast amounts of data from various systems, including seismic surveys, drilling logs, and equipment sensors. These datasets often come in different formats and structures, making it difficult to create a cohesive data environment. Engineers need to leverage data integration tools and techniques to harmonize these disparate sources, ensuring that AI algorithms have access to a comprehensive and unified dataset. This not only enhances the reliability of AI models but also facilitates more nuanced analyses that can drive better decision-making.

Availability of data is equally important, particularly in remote or offshore environments where data collection can be sporadic.

The challenges of connectivity and infrastructure in these locations can lead to significant gaps in data availability, impacting the performance of AI-driven systems. To mitigate these issues, companies must invest in robust data infrastructure that includes real-time data collection and transmission capabilities. Implementing edge computing solutions can also help by processing data closer to the source, reducing latency and ensuring that AI systems can operate with the most current information available.

Additionally, the dynamic nature of oil and gas operations necessitates ongoing data management strategies. As conditions change—whether due to variations in reservoir behavior, equipment performance, or environmental factors— AI models must adapt to these new realities. Continuous monitoring and updating of datasets are essential to maintain the relevance of predictive maintenance systems and enhance oil recovery techniques. Engineers and data scientists should establish protocols for regularly auditing and refreshing data to ensure that AI applications remain effective and aligned with the latest operational conditions.

Finally, fostering a culture of data stewardship across organizations can significantly enhance data quality and availability. Empowering teams to recognize the importance of accurate and timely data collection will lead to improved practices at all levels of operations. Training programs focused on data management best practices can equip employees with the skills necessary to maintain data integrity. By promoting a collaborative approach to data handling, companies can create a more resilient and efficient environment for leveraging AI innovations in exploration and production, ultimately driving better outcomes in the oil and gas industry.

Integration with Existing Systems

Integration with existing systems is a critical aspect of implementing AI innovations in the oil and gas sector. As companies strive to harness the power of artificial intelligence, they must ensure that these advanced technologies can seamlessly work with legacy systems that have been in use for decades. Many oil and gas operations rely on a complex network of equipment, data management solutions, and software applications that have evolved over time. A thoughtful integration approach can enhance operational efficiency and enable companies to leverage AI capabilities without disrupting their established workflows.

One of the primary challenges in integrating AI with existing systems is the varied nature of data formats and sources within the industry. Data is often generated from different sensors, equipment, and databases, each with its unique standards and formats. To facilitate successful integration, companies may need to invest in data normalization and transformation processes. This involves creating a unified framework that allows disparate data sources to communicate effectively. By doing so, engineers and scientists can ensure that AI algorithms have access to comprehensive datasets, thus improving predictive maintenance capabilities and enabling more accurate decision-making.

AI-driven exploration and drilling optimization also requires a robust integration strategy. Modern drilling operations generate vast amounts of data in real-time, including geological surveys, drilling parameters, and equipment performance metrics. Integrating AI systems with existing drilling management software allows for real-time analysis and insights, which can significantly enhance drilling efficiency. For instance, AI can analyze historical drilling data to predict the best drilling techniques or locations, thereby reducing costs and minimizing the risk of drilling failures. Successful integration not only improves operational outcomes but also ensures that engineers can make data-driven decisions based on real-time insights.

Enhanced oil recovery techniques can also benefit from strategic integration with existing systems. Traditional methods often involve complex workflows that can be difficult to modify. However, by integrating AI with existing reservoir management systems, companies can optimize recovery processes. AI algorithms can analyze patterns in reservoir behavior and recommend adjustments to extraction techniques. This integration allows engineers to implement AI-driven strategies without overhauling their entire operation, ensuring continuity and stability while benefiting from the advanced capabilities of AI.

In conclusion, the successful integration of AI innovations into existing oil and gas systems is essential for maximizing the benefits of these technologies. By overcoming challenges related to data compatibility, operational workflows, and the complexity of existing systems, companies can unlock new levels of efficiency and effectiveness in exploration and production. Engineers and scientists play a vital role in this integration process, as their expertise is crucial in aligning AI solutions with the nuanced requirements of the oil and gas industry. As organizations continue to adopt AI, the focus on integration will be paramount in realizing the full potential of these transformative technologies.

Skills Gap and Training Needs

The rapid integration of artificial intelligence in the oil and gas industry has highlighted a significant skills gap among the workforce. As companies increasingly adopt advanced technologies for exploration, production, and maintenance, the demand for professionals who possess both domain expertise and proficiency in AI applications continues to rise. Engineers and scientists in the sector must not only understand the traditional aspects of oil and gas operations but also be equipped with the knowledge of data analytics, machine learning algorithms, and AI-driven tools that enhance operational efficiency and decision-making processes.

Training needs assessment is crucial for bridging this skills gap. Organizations should conduct thorough evaluations to identify specific competencies that their workforce lacks in relation to AI technologies. This includes understanding how predictive maintenance algorithms can be effectively applied in oil rigs to minimize downtime and optimize asset performance. Engineers must learn about data collection methods, predictive modeling, and the interpretation of analytics to effectively utilize these advanced systems. Moreover, fostering a culture of continuous learning will empower employees to adapt to the rapidly changing technological landscape.

In the realm of AI-driven exploration and drilling optimization, personnel must be trained in advanced simulation techniques and geological data analysis. Engineers and scientists need to develop skills in utilizing AI to process vast amounts of geological and geophysical data, enabling them to uncover new drilling opportunities and optimize existing ones. Understanding the intricacies of AI algorithms that predict the best drilling locations and techniques is essential for maximizing resource extraction while minimizing environmental impact. Training programs should focus on hands-on experience with AI tools that facilitate real-time data analysis and decision support.

Enhanced oil recovery techniques using AI also require specialized training for engineers and scientists. With AI applications designed to optimize recovery processes, professionals must gain insights into machine learning models that analyze reservoir behavior and predict recovery outcomes. This necessitates a solid foundation in both geosciences and AI methodologies. Training initiatives should include collaborative workshops, interdisciplinary courses, and practical case studies that illustrate successful AI applications in enhanced oil recovery scenarios, emphasizing the importance of integrating AI with traditional engineering practices.

Finally, partnerships between industry stakeholders, academic institutions, and technology providers can play a pivotal role in addressing the skills gap. By fostering collaborative training programs and research initiatives, organizations can ensure that their workforce is well-equipped to navigate the complexities of AI technologies in oil and gas. Such partnerships can facilitate knowledge transfer, promote innovation, and ultimately enhance the industry's overall capability to leverage AI for improved efficiency and sustainability in exploration and production efforts.

Chapter 7: Future Trends in AI for Oil and Gas

Emerging AI Technologies

Emerging AI technologies are poised to revolutionize the oil and gas industry by enhancing operational efficiency and decision-making processes. As the sector faces increasing pressures to optimize production and reduce environmental impact, the integration of artificial intelligence into exploration and production workflows offers transformative solutions. Engineers and scientists are at the forefront of these innovations, leveraging advanced algorithms and machine learning techniques to analyze vast datasets, improve predictive capabilities, and streamline operations. This shift not only enhances productivity but also supports the industry's transition towards more sustainable practices.

Predictive maintenance, one of the most significant applications of AI in oil rigs, enables companies to anticipate equipment failures before they occur. By utilizing machine learning models trained on historical performance data, engineers can identify patterns that indicate potential malfunctions. This proactive approach minimizes downtime, reduces maintenance costs, and extends the lifespan of critical equipment. Furthermore, real-time monitoring systems equipped with AI can continuously assess the health of machinery, allowing for timely interventions that prevent costly disruptions in production.

AI-driven exploration techniques are also transforming how companies approach resource identification and extraction. Traditional methods often rely on geological surveys and historical drilling data, which can be time-consuming and inefficient. However, by employing AI algorithms that analyze geospatial data, seismic readings, and other relevant parameters, engineers can significantly enhance the accuracy of subsurface models. This technological advancement not only accelerates the discovery process but also minimizes the environmental footprint associated with exploratory drilling, aligning with the industry's sustainability goals.

Drilling optimization is another critical area where emerging AI technologies are making a substantial impact. Advanced AI systems can analyze drilling parameters in real-time to optimize drill bit performance and enhance penetration rates. By incorporating machine learning algorithms that adapt to varying geological conditions, engineers can achieve more efficient drilling practices, reducing both operational costs and the risk of non-productive time. This level of optimization directly contributes to maximizing resource recovery and ensures that drilling operations are conducted with greater precision and safety.

Finally, enhanced oil recovery techniques using AI are paving the way for improved extraction methods that can lead to increased production rates from existing fields. AI models can simulate reservoir behavior under different extraction scenarios, allowing engineers to identify the most effective strategies for maximizing output. Techniques such as data-driven reservoir modeling and machine learning optimization of injection strategies are becoming increasingly prevalent. As these technologies continue to evolve, they promise to unlock new potential in mature oil fields, ultimately driving efficiency and profitability in an ever-challenging market landscape.

Predictive Analytics and Big Data

Predictive analytics, powered by big data, is transforming the oil and gas industry by enabling companies to make data-driven decisions that enhance operational efficiency and reduce costs. By analyzing vast amounts of data collected from various sources, including sensors on drilling rigs, geological surveys, and historical production data, organizations can gain valuable insights into equipment performance, reservoir behavior, and market dynamics. This analytical approach not only assists in optimizing existing processes but also fosters innovation in exploration and production techniques. Engineers and scientists in the industry can leverage these insights to anticipate potential failures, optimize maintenance schedules, and improve overall asset management.

In the context of predictive maintenance for oil rigs, big data analytics plays a crucial role in minimizing downtime and maximizing productivity. By continuously monitoring equipment conditions through IoT sensors, companies can collect real-time data on machinery performance, identifying patterns and anomalies that may indicate impending failures. Predictive maintenance algorithms then analyze this data to forecast the likelihood of equipment breakdowns, allowing engineers to intervene proactively. This shift from reactive to predictive maintenance not only reduces operational costs associated with unplanned outages but also extends the lifespan of critical assets, thereby enhancing overall efficiency in oil and gas operations.

AI-driven exploration and drilling optimization represent another significant application of predictive analytics in the oil and gas sector. By integrating geological data, seismic surveys, and drilling parameters, predictive models can identify the most promising drilling locations and optimize the drilling process itself. Machine learning algorithms can analyze historical drilling data to refine drilling techniques, predict drilling outcomes, and minimize non-productive time. This capability not only accelerates the exploration phase but also reduces the environmental impact by optimizing resource extraction while maintaining safety standards. Engineers can utilize these insights to enhance decision-making processes, leading to more successful exploration ventures.

Enhanced oil recovery techniques are also witnessing a transformation through the application of predictive analytics and big data. By analyzing reservoir data and fluid dynamics, predictive models can help identify the most effective recovery methods tailored to specific reservoir conditions. For instance, machine learning can be used to analyze the effectiveness of various injection strategies, enabling engineers to optimize water flooding, gas injection, or chemical processes. Such targeted approaches to enhanced oil recovery not only improve production rates but also contribute to more sustainable practices by minimizing waste and enhancing the overall efficiency of resource extraction.

The integration of predictive analytics and big data within the oil and gas sector is reshaping the landscape of exploration and production. As engineers and scientists continue to harness the potential of AI technologies, the industry is poised to achieve unprecedented levels of efficiency, safety, and sustainability. By embracing these innovations, professionals can navigate the complexities of modern oil and gas operations while positioning their organizations for future success in a rapidly evolving energy landscape. The ongoing advancements in predictive analytics will undoubtedly play a pivotal role in driving the next wave of innovation within the industry.

The Role of AI in Sustainable Practices

The integration of artificial intelligence (AI) in sustainable practices within the oil and gas industry has emerged as a transformative force, significantly enhancing operational efficiency and environmental stewardship. AI technologies facilitate data analysis at unprecedented scales, allowing companies to assess resource management, emissions, and energy consumption with greater accuracy. By leveraging machine learning algorithms, organizations can predict equipment failures and optimize processes, ultimately reducing their environmental footprint while maintaining productivity. This capability is particularly critical in an industry that faces increasing scrutiny over its impact on climate change and natural resources.

Predictive maintenance is one of the most compelling applications of AI in promoting sustainability in oil and gas operations. By utilizing real-time data from various sensors on equipment, AI systems can forecast when a component is likely to fail, enabling proactive maintenance actions. This not only minimizes downtime and costly repairs but also ensures that equipment operates at optimal efficiency. When machinery runs smoothly, fuel consumption and emissions are significantly reduced, contributing to a smaller carbon footprint. The proactive nature of predictive maintenance aligns with sustainable practices by extending the life of assets and minimizing waste.

AI-driven exploration and drilling optimization represent another crucial aspect of sustainable practices in the sector.

Traditional exploration methods often involve extensive land use and resource extraction, which can lead to significant environmental degradation. However, AI technologies can analyze geological data to identify the most promising drilling sites, optimizing the use of resources and minimizing the disturbance to ecosystems. By employing algorithms that process seismic data and historical drilling performance, companies can make informed decisions that reduce the number of exploratory wells, thereby conserving land and reducing the potential for environmental harm.

Enhanced oil recovery techniques powered by AI further contribute to sustainability efforts within the industry. These techniques focus on maximizing the extraction of oil while minimizing waste and environmental impact. AI can analyze reservoir data to identify the most effective recovery methods, such as water flooding or gas injection, tailored to specific geological conditions. This targeted approach not only enhances recovery rates but also reduces the amount of energy and resources expended in the extraction process. By improving the efficiency of oil recovery, companies can produce more energy with less environmental impact, aligning their operations with global sustainability goals.

In conclusion, the role of AI in sustainable practices within the oil and gas industry is multifaceted and impactful. From predictive maintenance that enhances equipment efficiency to AI-driven exploration that conserves resources and minimizes environmental disruption, the technology serves as a powerful ally in the pursuit of sustainability. Enhanced recovery techniques further underscore AI's potential to facilitate responsible resource extraction. As the industry continues to evolve, the integration of AI will be crucial in balancing the demand for energy with the imperative to protect the environment, ensuring a sustainable future for the sector.

Chapter 8: Conclusion

Summary of Key Innovations

The oil and gas industry has witnessed significant advancements through the integration of artificial intelligence, leading to transformative changes in exploration and production processes. Key innovations in this sector have primarily focused on enhancing operational efficiency, reducing downtime, and optimizing resource extraction. The deployment of sophisticated algorithms and machine learning techniques has enabled companies to analyze vast amounts of data in real-time, facilitating better decision-making and improved asset management.

Predictive maintenance has emerged as a critical innovation, particularly in oil rigs, where equipment failure can result in substantial financial losses and safety hazards. By leveraging AI and machine learning, companies can monitor the health of machinery, predict failures before they occur, and schedule maintenance activities more effectively. This proactive approach not only minimizes unplanned downtime but also extends the lifespan of equipment, leading to significant cost savings and enhanced operational reliability.

AI-driven exploration techniques have revolutionized the way geoscientists and engineers approach the search for oil and gas reserves. Advanced data analytics and machine learning algorithms are now employed to interpret geological data, identify potential drilling sites, and assess the viability of exploration projects. These innovations allow for more accurate predictions regarding the location and size of hydrocarbon deposits, reducing the risks associated with exploration and enabling more targeted and efficient drilling operations.

In the realm of drilling optimization, AI technologies are optimizing drilling parameters and processes to enhance efficiency and reduce costs. Smart drilling systems, powered by real-time data analytics, can automatically adjust drilling parameters based on subsurface conditions, ensuring optimal performance. This dynamic adaptability leads to improved drilling rates and reduced non-productive time, ultimately lowering the overall costs associated with exploration and production.

Enhanced oil recovery techniques utilizing AI are paving the way for more efficient extraction methods. By modeling reservoir behavior and simulating various recovery scenarios, AI systems can identify the most effective techniques for maximizing oil recovery from existing fields. This innovative approach not only increases production levels but also minimizes environmental impacts by reducing the need for new drilling sites. As these AI innovations continue to evolve, they hold the potential to redefine the future of the oil and gas industry, driving productivity and sustainability efforts.

The Future of AI in the Oil and Gas Sector

The future of artificial intelligence in the oil and gas sector is poised to reshape the landscape of exploration, production, and maintenance. With the industry's increasing reliance on data-driven decision-making, AI technologies such as machine learning, deep learning, and advanced analytics are becoming essential tools for engineers and scientists. These technologies allow for the processing of vast amounts of geological, operational, and economic data, enabling companies to make more informed choices that enhance efficiency and reduce costs. As the sector evolves, the integration of AI will not only streamline operations but also facilitate more sustainable practices, addressing environmental concerns while meeting energy demands.

Predictive maintenance is one of the most promising applications of AI in oil rigs. By leveraging machine learning algorithms, companies can analyze historical maintenance data and real-time sensor information to predict equipment failures before they occur. This proactive approach minimizes downtime and maintenance costs, ensuring that operations run smoothly. Engineers can implement AI-driven monitoring systems that track the health of critical components, allowing for timely interventions and optimizing maintenance schedules. The result is a more reliable and efficient operation, which is vital in an industry where unplanned outages can lead to significant financial losses.

AI-driven exploration and drilling optimization represent a significant advancement in the quest for new oil reserves. Advanced algorithms can analyze geological data and seismic surveys with greater accuracy than traditional methods, identifying potential drilling sites more effectively. Machine learning models can predict the likelihood of encountering oil and gas deposits based on historical drilling data, allowing engineers to prioritize high-potential areas. Furthermore, real-time data analysis during drilling operations enables adaptive drilling strategies, optimizing parameters such as pressure and rotation speed, which enhances drilling efficiency and reduces costs.

Enhanced oil recovery techniques are also being transformed by AI technologies. By utilizing data analytics, engineers can better understand reservoir behavior and fluid dynamics, leading to more effective recovery strategies. AI models can simulate various recovery techniques and predict their outcomes, allowing for the selection of the most efficient methods. Moreover, AI can enhance the implementation of techniques such as CO_2 injection or thermal recovery by optimizing the conditions under which these processes are performed. This not only improves yield but also contributes to more sustainable practices by maximizing resource utilization and minimizing waste.

In conclusion, the integration of AI in the oil and gas sector heralds a new era of innovation that promises to enhance productivity and sustainability. As engineers and scientists continue to harness the power of AI, the industry will benefit from improved predictive maintenance, optimized exploration and drilling processes, and advanced recovery techniques. The ongoing evolution of AI technologies will enable the sector to adapt to the challenges of a changing energy landscape, ensuring that oil and gas companies remain competitive while addressing environmental responsibilities. The future holds immense potential for those willing to embrace these advancements and leverage them for transformative outcomes.

Final Thoughts and Recommendations

As the oil and gas industry continues to navigate the complexities of modern energy demands, the integration of artificial intelligence presents unprecedented opportunities for innovation and efficiency. Engineers and scientists must recognize that AI technologies are not merely tools but rather transformative agents capable of reshaping exploration and production processes. Embracing AI can lead to improved decision-making, enhanced safety measures, and optimized resource management, ultimately driving profitability and sustainability in operations.

In the realm of predictive maintenance, AI's ability to analyze vast datasets can significantly reduce downtime and maintenance costs on oil rigs. By employing machine learning algorithms, operators can predict equipment failures before they occur, allowing for timely interventions and minimizing disruptions to production. It is essential for professionals in the field to invest in AI-driven predictive maintenance systems and cultivate a culture that values proactive asset management, ensuring that the workforce is trained to leverage these technologies effectively.

AI-driven exploration and drilling optimization represents another critical area where engineers and scientists can make substantial advancements. By utilizing advanced data analytics and simulation models, oil and gas companies can enhance their exploration strategies, identifying potential drilling sites with greater precision and reducing the risks associated with exploration. Professionals should advocate for the adoption of AI solutions that analyze geological data, seismic readings, and historical drilling performance, enabling more informed decision-making and efficient resource allocation.

Furthermore, enhanced oil recovery techniques utilizing AI can unlock significant reserves that would otherwise remain untapped. Machine learning algorithms can optimize injection strategies and analyze reservoir behavior, leading to increased recovery rates and improved economic viability of oil fields. Engineers and scientists must prioritize research and collaboration in this area, sharing insights and best practices to drive innovation and achieve breakthroughs in recovery methods.

In conclusion, the potential of AI innovations in oil and gas is vast and multifaceted. For engineers and scientists, the pathway to harnessing this potential lies in a commitment to continuous learning and adaptation. By actively engaging with emerging AI technologies, advocating for their implementation, and collaborating with interdisciplinary teams, professionals can lead the charge in transforming the industry. Embracing these changes will not only enhance operational efficiency but also position the sector for a sustainable future amid evolving energy landscapes.